THE FACE
OF
AMERICA

THE FACE
OF
AMERICA

BY THE EDITORS OF
THE SATURDAY EVENING POST

THE CURTIS PUBLISHING COMPANY
PHILADELPHIA

DOUBLEDAY & COMPANY, INC.
GARDEN CITY

THE FACE OF

AMERICA

AN INTRODUCTION

BY PAUL HORGAN

THE SPIRIT OF A FREE NATION is composed
about equally of its memories and its hopes—that is to say, its history
and the lasting faith by which it was founded.

Each generation of the United States opens its eyes
upon new images of these old enduring values. They are born anew
with every child who comes to our life. His image of what he first sees is
forever after his America, no matter how the conditions of his world
may change with the passage of his lifetime. In his years, he is a maker
of the present, and in his belief he is a creator of the future.

Whatever the immediate terms or rewards of his place in our life
and our work as a people, he partakes of a larger vision than that
of his local place and his daily job. It is this which makes him
a transcontinental citizen of this country, even while he throws himself
with ingenious energy into the challenge of contributing his own personality
and vocation to the character of the place where he was born,

or, if he chooses to move, the place where he decides to live.

He is an American, enfranchised by the Constitution, and animated

by his freedom to be who he is, subject only to restraints invented by all

for the benefit of each. He is like a craftsman free to cast a likeness

in bronze of the subject he knows best—the citizen of the United States,

for which he, as himself, must be the model.

But this image, or another of the same meaning, is a private one,

held within, and almost never told outward. The sense of his nation

openly admitted, and broadly shared, comes free in another way. It is a way

cheerfully diffuse and various. It has as many images as we have kinds

of country and ways of work and styles of play. These are what we see when

we go about our days and nights, living at home, or traveling across our states.

These are what the pages of this book have captured, in pictures

that give back to us many materials of our common experience and memory.

Here, then, is the aggregate of how we are in that continental

neighborhood which is our part of North America.

It is a neighborhood so big that hardly any of us can know

everything about the rest of us—and yet we know the essential thing

which we hold in common. It has many faces. It is the beauty of this land

given into our care. It is the way we work. It is the way we worship;

the way we play and the way we remember. It is the long shadow

cast westward across the continent by our sunrise in our youth

among nations, and it is the duty shown to us by that light

as we mature amidst the older peoples of the world. It is the enduring

spirit of the United States, which separately each of us defines for himself;

and it is the vast act of our common life which we all perform together.

That spirit and that act shine forth in this composite portrait of

THE FACE OF AMERICA.

THE FACE OF
AMERICA
IN
SPRING

THE BRANDYWINE IN SPRING

The Brandywine, a jewel among rivers, is so small that map makers call it a creek. But it looms large in American history, poetry and art. Lovely in all seasons, "the bright, the laughing Brandywine" is seen here at its best, wreathed in dogwood and redbud blossoms. The time is early May; the occasion, an outing of the Wilmington Trail Club at a river bend near Rockland, Delaware. A few miles south of here, the Brandywine courses through Wilmington, joins the Christina River, and empties into the broad Delaware. The estuary was discovered by Swedish colonists in 1638. Later on, Quaker settlers found the river's twin-branch sources, sixty miles north in Pennsylvania. And much later, in 1777, their great-great-grandsons saw a Revolutionary army outflanked and beaten in the Battle of the Brandywine; the British command knew of more fords than Washington did. During the next half century, water wheels on the Brandywine ran famous mills. Paper, flour and textiles were made here, and the first DuPont gunpowder. Steam engines ended all that. But ancient dams and millsites are still to be seen, overgrown now with ash, sycamore and tall oaks.

Photograph by Frank Ross

CHERRY-BLOSSOM TIME

Once again spring comes up from the south, and cherry trees blush at her velvety kiss. The Japanese cherries massed in Washington's Potomac Park also symbolize man's hope of peace, for these were given in friendship by the City of Tokyo. The transplanting was not easy. First, scions from several types of flowering trees were propagated at the

Okitsu Imperial Horticultural Experimental Station, a painstaking job begun in 1910.
All were then grafted on wild cherry root stock. In March, 1912, a thousand saplings reached Washington. Six hundred single-flowering Yoshino cherries were planted around the Tidal Basin, now overlooked by the Jefferson Memorial. The rest were double-flowering types—Fugenzo, Fukurokugu and Kwanzon—and were set out along the Park's curving drives. The Yoshinos bloom in late March or early April, depending on the weather, and the other varieties follow. When the Kwanzons' pink glory finally fades to white, the show is over . . . until next year.

Photograph by Ivan Dmitri

RITES OF SPRING

What's this? Surely not baseball? It is,
indeed, that time of year again.
Nowadays baseball starts in March to
the accompaniment of tropical breezes and
waving palm trees, and pretty soon the
players move northward. The rites of spring
training, first performed in the 1880's,
have become as much a part of baseball as
night games and Sunday double-headers.
Most clubs pitch their training camps
in Florida, and happy, indeed, is the town
that has a team to attract the thousands
of baseball-starved fans who come
to look upon the players during their
preseason unlimbering. Here you see the
Chicago White Sox in a workout
at Fort Myers, Florida, shortly before
they took on the Pittsburgh Pirates
one day in March of 1955. The Pirates,
who train at Fort Myers, won 7–6, and went
on to top the whole "Grapefruit League"—
a very hot team, it seemed. But, alas,
it didn't mean a thing. When the season
ended in September the Pirates had sunk
to the bottom of the National League
as almost everybody had predicted.

12   *Photograph by Frank Ross*

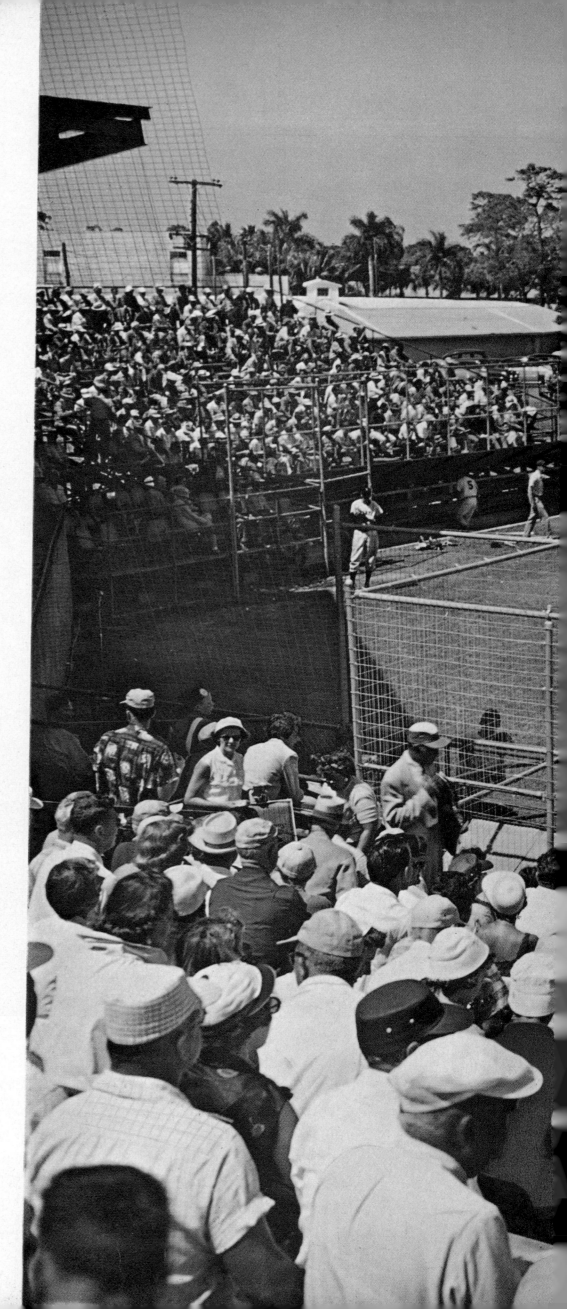

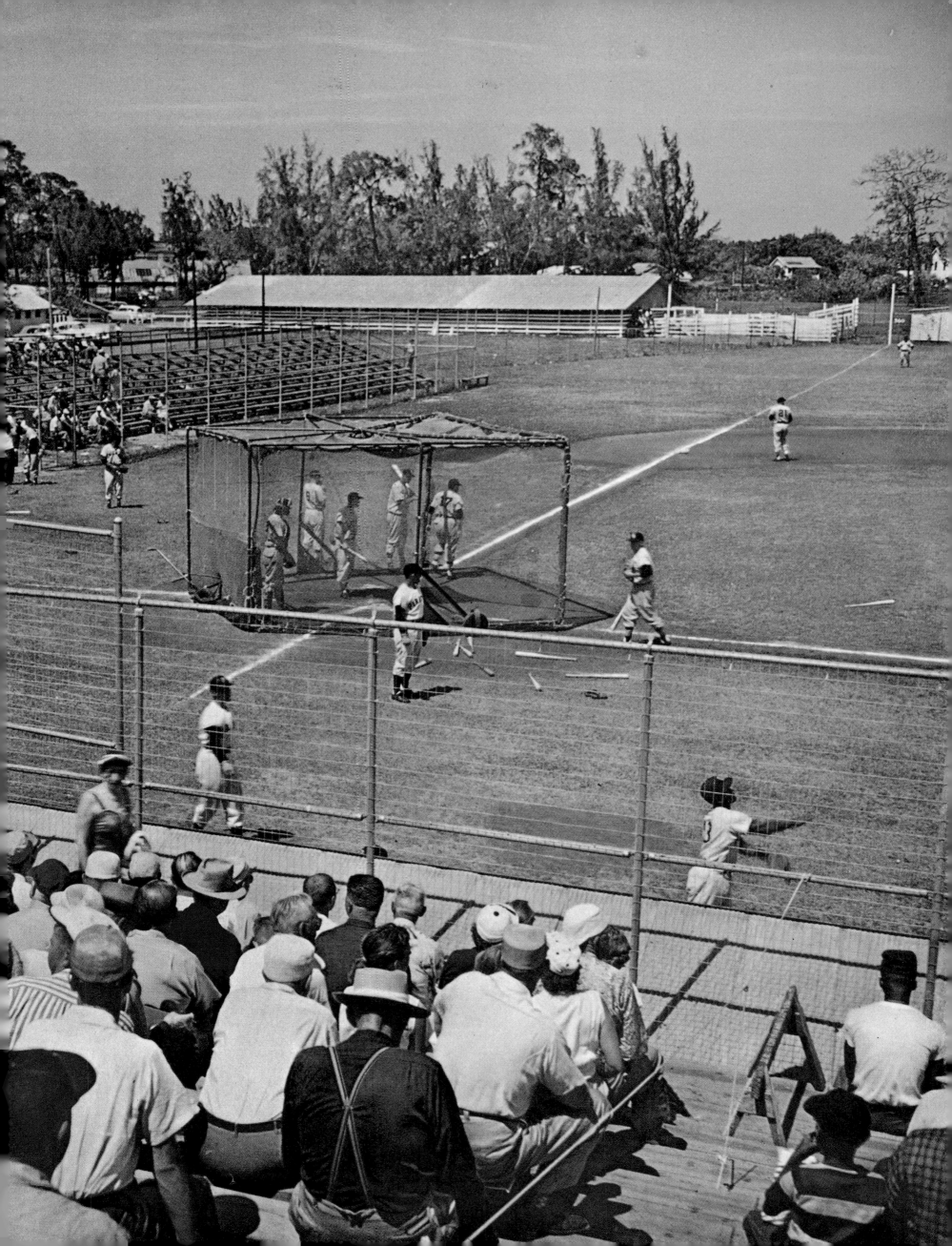

MELLOW MISSION

For generations, the doves of San Juan
Capistrano have played second fiddle
to the well-publicized swallows that
return here each year on the nineteenth
of March. The peregrinating swallows
are regular visitors, but the
more loyal doves never leave.
Here, at the Fountain of the Doves,
friendly white waddlers welcome tourists
and flutter prettily in hope of handouts.
Behind the fountain stands a statue of
Father Junipero Serra, who founded this
mission 180 years ago. By 1812, Capistrano
was one of the loveliest and strongest links
in a chain of Franciscan establishments
along the coast of old California.
That year, however, a violent earthquake
destroyed the mission's magnificent church
(entombing twoscore Indian converts at worship).
Rebuilding progresses today, slowly,
patiently and at great expense.
It may be another century
before the restoration is complete.
But the doves and swallows couldn't care less.
They love Capistrano just the way it is.

Photograph by Sid Avery   15

SPRING IN THE SMOKIES

Spring has sprung, and the earth adorns herself in pristine finery. Here at Walnut Bottom on Big Creek, in the North Carolina part of the Great Smoky Mountains National Park, nature lovers perform traditional rites with camera and tripod. Along with almost a thousand others from twenty-seven states and five foreign countries, they motor and hike through the Annual Spring Wildflower Pilgrimage of the Great Smokies. A deep carpet of fringed phacelia soothes the weary feet of hardy enthusiasts who may tramp eleven miles horizontally and 4900 feet vertically in an afternoon, pursuing doll's-eyes (*Actaea brachypoda*) or hearts-bustin'-with-love (*Euonymus americanus*), both of which bloom in the park. Official guides accompany the tours to identify the growing things and to make sure that no one picks the flowers.

Photograph by Larry Keighley

OVER THE WALL

Horses and riders from various parts of the world
competed in the equestrian events of the
Olympic Games at Stockholm in June, 1956.
The United States was represented by eight men
and ten horses chosen after a year-long
competition. The spectators shown here are seated
on a hillside at Tryon, North Carolina,
watching the final tryouts, in March, in which
Frank Chapot rides his chestnut gelding
Belair over a formidable brick wall, one of
the many difficult obstacles encountered in the
competition for the Prix des Nations event
for jumpers. Other contestants were entered in
the Three Day event, the world's most demanding
test of a horse, which involves training,
a twenty-mile cross-country endurance ride and
show-ring jumping. Training and mounting
an equestrian team is an expensive venture,
wholly supported by personal subscriptions from
people interested in horses—the United States
team receives nothing from the Olympic
Committee. Five members of our team were
civilians and the three others, including
Frank Chapot, were on detached service from
the Armed Forces. Managing the team was
Brig. Gen. John Tupper Cole, one of
the mainstays of the United States team
when this country still had cavalry.

WATERY WILDERNESS

Beneath gray shrouds of Spanish moss, a Cajun couple paddle across the dark, still waters of Bayou Chicot. Overhead, the boughs of gum trees and tall cypresses shield them from the Louisiana sun. It is a pleasant spring Sunday here, about 75 miles (as the crow flies) northwest of Baton Rouge. Like many of the inhabitants of Evangeline Parish who enjoy boating on the lake, Doc Wiggins and his wife are descendants of the Nova Scotia Acadians whose exile to Louisiana two centuries ago inspired Longfellow to create his ill-fated heroine. From her, the parish took its name. Once a swampy, cut-over area, Bayou Chicot is now a well-cared-for state park. To the Choctaw Indians, this kind of waterway was a *bayuk*, or small river. But to early settlers trying hard to capture the meandering tranquillity of the tree-studded lakes, a bayou was known as "the place of the sleeping water."

20 *Photograph by Ivan Dmitri*

HIGH CLIMBER

A moment after the tip of this tree snapped free, the trimmed trunk whipped back and forth. Up at the top, riding out the frenzied lashing, was Loren "Dutch" Streeter, a "high climber" or "tree topper" for the St. Paul & Tacoma Lumber Company. During logging operations in the Northwest a tall, straight "spar" tree is left standing. Then the tree topper works his way up, trimming branches with ax and saw. At a height of about 175 feet, Streeter tops the tree, hoping a freakish wind won't blow it the wrong way or that the trunk won't split along its length as the tip breaks off. After Streeter descends, rigging equipment is attached to the spar tree so that trees already felled can be dragged to loading points. Streeter's work is dangerous, but, riding high in the sky, he sees some fine scenery. That's Mount Rainier in the background.

Photograph by Bob and Ira Spring

ENDURING BEAUTY

Two hundred years ago young Henry Middleton had 800 slaves and 50,000 acres. Like Nebuchadnezzar of Babylon, he ordered his slaves to build a garden. They toiled for ten years on the bank of the Ashley, twelve miles above Charleston in South Carolina, and Henry's garden became famous—even in the Old World. A second Henry planted four camellias. Three still thrive, after 150 years. A Middleton named Williams planted azaleas around the pool. A marble nymph contemplates them while she ties her sandal. Succeeding generations of Middletons carried on. Now tourists are welcome to stroll the garden's paths—for a fee. Middleton Place today lacks only a Middleton. But the owner, J. J. Pringle Smith, has Middleton blood. Recently he added 35,000 more azaleas.

Photograph by Harland Sutherland—Kabel Photos   25

AMERICANS ALL

This day they swear to defend the United States against all enemies. At the District Court in Washington, D. C., 141 subjects of thirty-two foreign nations become Americans. Wladimir the Ukrainian becomes a U. S. citizen named Walter, and Szymon the Pole plain Simon. Feige from Russia will answer to Fannie, and Liu Chia-Len to Bill. Little Dan Vega stands between Air Force Major Carl Vega and his wife, who adopted Dan in Germany and now pledge fealty to his new country on his behalf. It was a roundabout road, but Dan made it—he's an American kid now. The strength of the United States will insure the rights of the Constitution to each of these 141 persons. Each owes a new allegiance which he accepts "without purpose of evasion." The clerk of the court intones the oath, and a dream comes true.

26   *Photograph by Frank Ross*

LOG DRIVE

Down from Idaho's high forests comes raw
stuff for America's builders—Douglas fir,
ponderosa pine, spruce, red cedar, white pine.
Here several of the 34-man river crew
battle a "center," the most dangerous type
of jam—hung on a mid-river bar,
touching neither bank. When logs are
beyond the reach of shorebound tractors,
men shod with calks and armed with
twelve-pound peaveys must pry loose
the pile-up before the river chokes.
If the drivers fail, dynamiters blast—
and incidentally destroy much of
the valuable timber, which is destined
for the Potlatch Forests mills at
Lewiston on the Clearwater. As roads
and trucks invade the receding
forests, the race of river drivers is
vanishing from the face of America
and one day will remain only as
legend. Meantime, you can still hear
them yell "She rides!" whenever
a jam breaks and one-to-three-ton logs
churn the water white in headlong fury.
The timber comes out once again, courtesy
of the toughest boys on the river.

UNDER GOD'S SKY

The prayer soon to be offered by Archbishop
Joseph P. Hurley, now at the altar, will
mark the most significant moment in the lives of
the four young men wearing long white albs.
The occasion is the first Roman Catholic ordination
ever held out-of-doors in the United States.
The setting—St. Augustine's Mission of
Nombre de Dios on a Sunday in May—is a
fitting one: This ground, shaded by cedar trees
and a canopy of Spanish moss, is the site
of the first parish Mass ever celebrated
in this country. The year was 1565,
just after Don Pedro Menéndez de Avilés
had established a colony here in the name of
Philip II of Spain. Menéndez wouldn't know
St. Augustine today, but the ancient supplication
offered in Latin by Archbishop Hurley
has remained unchanged: "We beseech Thee,
almighty Father, invest these Thy servants
with the dignity of the priesthood . . ."
(*Da, quaesumus, omnipotens Pater,
in hos famulos tuos Presbyterii dignitatem . . .*)

Photograph by F. V. Rahner, Jr.

HIGH STEEL

Construction workers eat when the whistle blows.
If they happen to be on a girder thirty stories
above Lexington Avenue in New York City,
they have lunch with a view. On the left is
Louis Deer, a Mohawk Indian from Canada
who works in New York, where he can
draw $3.95 an hour for his nerve and skill.
With him is Monte Farrell, the "walking boss."
Monte does the leg work for the foreman,
who presides below. High-steel work is in
Monte's blood: his father helped put up the
Empire State Building, the Chrysler Building
and the George Washington Bridge. But Monte
admits that building towers into the sky
"is enough to put gray hairs on anyone's head,"
and he hopes his son will become an engineer.
This stark skyscraper skeleton is that of a
$20,000,000 building called simply 485 Lexington
Avenue. By early fall, it was fleshed with
concrete, glass and modern décor; an
advertising agency's craftsmen now ply their
hectic trade where Louis and Monte
worked placidly. Perhaps by now the unsung
hero of this picture, the photographer, is
his old self again. He had to do his shutter-
snapping and film-changing while perched on
one of those girders. "I was really shook,"
he said when he came back to earth.

32   *Photograph by Larry Fried*

SONG OF THE OHIO

That's the Ohio—lazy twisty river that runs from
Pittsburgh a thousand miles to Cairo on the Mississippi.
This side's Kentucky. Over there, Indiana. Lazy?
She gets wild sometimes, rears up with a yellow look—
and watch out, captain, Cincinnati's cresting
eighty feet. In June she's gentle—like that summer
of 1816, right about here, near Hawesville.

Tom and Nancy Lincoln and their boy Abe ferried across. Tom hadn't been doing well at carpentering in Kentucky. Indiana wasn't any better. Poor Nancy died, and Tom never did do well, but Abe grew up and did fine. Abe flat-boated on this river. When he was a boy and long after, packet boat was king. Now sassy tugboats push cargo barges.

Nine-foot channel—the Engineers ripped out the snags. Still, the river has a few tricks left. The Ohio's old and sly. She's carried the pirogues of the Sieur de la Salle and destroyers bound for destiny in the Orient. Just don't trust her too far. She'll work for you a hundred years, then drown you in a fit.

Photograph by Frank Ross

UP IN FLAMES

The morning of May twenty-first was clear and cool,
a perfect day out at Russell Olson's 640-acre
Rolling Acres farm, near Bassett, Wisconsin.
But at 9:30 A.M. Olson saw smoke pouring out
of his huge four-story, ultramodern barn, heard the
terrified bellowing of a purebred Hereford bull
that was inside. The bull was rescued, but the barn,
packed with 160 tons of hay, went up like a torch,
spewing flames 150 feet into the sky. Five
volunteer fire companies, from the nearby towns
of Antioch, Silver Lake, Twin Lakes, Trevor
and Wilmot, battled the fire for twenty-four
hours and, said farmer Olson gratefully, "did a
wonderful job." Although the $192,000 barn was
leveled and two of the four silos were badly
damaged, the fire laddies had saved his home,
a granary, a corncrib, a bull barn and a machinery
shed—another example of the fine work done
any hour, any day, by the members of the 12,000
volunteer fire companies around the country.

Photographs by Appel Color Photography   37

ARIZONA RANCH

South of the Gila in Apache country lies
Bellota Ranch, where Dick Reeve and
his wife run cattle. Tucson is twenty-five
miles west. It's half that far to a telephone.
Cowpunching here isn't mechanized.
The cow ponies are quarter-horse bred, stocky,
heavily muscled, with a touch of Arab—and
usually a cross of Thoroughbred. Fast?
Greased lightning—for a quarter mile. That's
how they got their name. Ranching is
lonely, free and independent. Power failure?
It's *your* generator—fix it. Your house is
built of earth—adobe, like the Reeves', there
beyond the corral. A style the Moors took
to Spain, Spaniards took to America,
Americans take anywhere: ranch house.
Pat Winter and her husband are up to visit
the Reeves. Pat's riding the palomino, sizing
up the stock. There's a track in Tucson.
Some races for Thoroughbreds, others
for quarter horses. Short races, but
exciting. A man said, "The horse players
get a chance to yell just three times."

38   *Photograph by Bill Shrout*

THE
GOLDEN TRIANGLE

This pie-shaped wedge of land lies between the
Monongahela (right) and Allegheny rivers where they
join to form the westing Ohio. Here, in 1758 rose
Fort Pitt and the frontier settlement of Pittsburgh, city
of coal, iron and sweat which was to become a gateway
to the industrial age. The land between the rivers,

known as the Golden Triangle for the immense
wealth it produced, lay grimed under a
pall of smoke. But Pittsburgh learned
to control her smog, and now the point of the
Triangle, where old Fort Pitt stood,
has been cleared of its clutter of old buildings.

It will soon be a tree-lined park. Behind this
stands Gateway Center, a new district of
shining stainless steel, aluminum and glass buildings.
Through a new kind of pioneering, the Triangle
is becoming a bright new gateway to the future.

Photograph by J. Alex Langley

41

IN MEMORIAM

From Arlington to remote prairie shrines to foreign fields,
America provides resting places for her fallen sons.
Now, on this poignant thirtieth day of May,
we revive the memory of heroes with living blossoms.
Jimmy Collins was a long way from home
when a Japanese machine gun cut him down in 1944.
He died in New Guinea, at twenty-seven, then
returned to lie forever in Kansas earth. Each year on
Memorial Day his father and mother drive seventy miles
from their farm to Fort Scott National Cemetery.
With Jimmy's parents in this photograph are three little
Collinses who also came to honor the uncle they never
knew. Long after the agony of Bunker Hill, Bull Run and
Bastogne, the dead lie in peace. They and their comrades
have left us names the world can never forget—
Shiloh, Château-Thierry, Iwo Jima, the Normandy
beachhead and the Pusan Perimeter. We gave the ground
they lie in; they hallow it. Afternoon shadows lengthen on
Memorial Day, somewhere faintly a bugle blows taps, and
we renew the resolve Abraham Lincoln bequeathed us—
that "these dead shall not have died in vain."

Photograph by Bill Shrout

THE FACE OF
AMERICA
IN
SUMMER

THE OLD MILL

Wolf Pen Mill, only twelve miles from bustling
Louisville, Kentucky, is generations removed from
modern city life. A young widow, Mrs. Robin Cooper,
bought the property in 1925. "Friends said I was
a lunatic to go live 'way out in the country," says
Mrs. Cooper, who still makes her home here. At the time
she acquired it, the rustic old building was in disrepair,
the pond filled with debris, the water wheel rotten.
Today, the painstakingly restored mill is again grinding
out corn meal as it did more than a century ago.
Even earlier, the Wolf Pen got its name from settlers
who trapped a pack of marauding wolves in the dell
at the foot of the falls and wiped them out.
The pond that now covers the site of the slaughter
is a favorite fishing hole for Mrs. Cooper's grandchildren,
Rebel, Roddy and Robin. The young anglers
catch only catfish and orphan bass fingerlings
that slip through the water gate, but they couldn't
be prouder if they hooked rainbow trout.
And when they arrive, as children inevitably must,
at the toilsome, worrisome state of adulthood,
what sweeter memories will they look back upon than
those summer afternoons by Wolf Pen Mill?

ETERNAL CANYON

No river dug a bigger bed than the Colorado's in Arizona.
Other canyons are called grand, but only one
is *The* Grand Canyon. Nearly 300 miles long,
over a mile deep—a superbomb's gouge is a pinprick
beside this hole in the ground. The patient river
has carved a façade that poets have failed to describe.
It worked in secret, still shuns intruders. Its rapids
have killed many. Undiscovered human bones
lie in its deeps, on its banks. But the canyon's
primitive beauty is accessible. The dour indomitable
mules of Arizona drovers take visitors—including
women and children—to the river's edge.
Switchback trails descend through the geologic ages,
like Dante's path into hell. At times the canyon has
infernal aspects—dead red earth under burning sun,
shadows that move as fast as a strolling man.
At others, it glows in celestial pinks, buffs and blues.
John Bradley's mules are bringing tourists up the
Kaibab Trail to the south rim at Windy Point, after
a night at Phantom Ranch, a canyon guest house.
The riders have seen earth that was before man—
violent as in the Creation. Geologists consider the
Grand Canyon relatively new. Scarcely a million years old.

Photograph by Bill Shrout

SUNSET PARADE

One March morning in 1801, about three weeks
after he moved into the White House,
President Thomas Jefferson set out on horseback
with Lieut. Col. William Ward Burrows,
commandant of the U. S. Marine Corps, to find a
suitable site upon which to build barracks for
the marines, who had recently arrived from the old
capital at Philadelphia. Here you see the spot
Jefferson chose because it "lay near the Navy Yard
and within easy marching distance of the
Capitol." One hundred and fifty-six years and
eighteen commandants later, some marines—but
no longer all of them—still inhabit the same
quiet quadrangle, and each Friday afternoon from
April until November the Marine Band, the
Drum and Bugle Corps and the headquarters drill
platoons stage a colorful "sunset parade" which
lasts for precisely forty minutes. The house
at the end of the parade grounds, to the left
of the barracks, is the home of the commandant
(currently General Randolph McC. Pate).
When the British sacked Washington in 1814
they spared this house, which permits the claim
that it is the oldest Federal building in the city
in continuous use. But, according to Marine Corps
legend, Brig. Gen. Archibald Henderson lived
there so long he forgot it belonged to the
Government and willed it to his son.
When Henderson died in 1859 he had been
commandant of the corps for thirty-eight years.

50   *Photograph by Larry Keighley*

BLUER
THAN THE SKY

The theme is beauty, and it's too bad this can't be a
panorama of all the moods of our land's beauty.
Or maybe it's not too bad. Our color-shifting
peaks, our many-humored oceans, the prairies,
the deserts, a city's electric-jeweled sky line
beneath the moon—maybe these can fully be savored
only separately, one by one. So here is just a field.
  The field is jealous of the blue sky and has
clothed itself in bluer wild lupine. In between,
green hills and russet earth and trees bearing pears
and plums, apricots and oranges go about being lovely
in their gentler ways. Well, a photographer comes
along, and three ladies are in the field, a bonus
of beauty, to be sure. Let's imagine a highway
sign is in the picture, saying: Upper Suisun Valley,
California—then, having read it, imagine the sign away.

52

Photograph by Glen Fishbach

TIP OF MANHATTAN

Down by the sea wall of lower Manhattan
there's always a free show: A never-ending parade of
freighters, ferries, tugs and ocean liners. Front-row center
seats for the spectacle are available at Battery Park,
a historic piece of real estate thrust into the Bay
of New York, where the Hudson meets the East River,
and on summer Tuesdays the park offers a band concert
staged on the mall of Castle Clinton. In the past,
before it became a national monument, the
Castle served as a fort, an opera house, a depot
through which 8,000,000 immigrants passed, and
an aquarium. On this particular Tuesday the
New York Fire Department band celebrates
Fire Fighters' Day on the mall. The spanking new
fireboat John D. McKean adds a spectacular,
watery salute to the festivities, a final fitting touch
to a show that Broadway couldn't beat.

54

Photograph by Maynard Clark

SYMPHONY IN CANVAS

The sloops round the buoy in a race off Marblehead,
Massachusetts. Close-hauled with a fresh breeze
off the port bow, they reach to windward. At the skipper's
command, the graceful vessels heel far over, catching
the wind on the starboard tack for the next leg.
The yacht at far right is just completing this maneuver,
a true test of a racing yacht's ability—and of her
helmsman's seamanship. Long before we dreamed of
burning the earth's substance to get energy for steamships
and nuclear-powered submarines, we learned to help
ourselves to wind power. Sailors have striven to
harness the most capricious force in nature with every
conceivable sort of ship, from crude Phoenician
rigs to the superb American clippers. By the 1850's
we could cross the Atlantic under sail alone in two weeks.
The fastest liners afloat today have cut that time to four days—
with the help of many tens of thousands of horsepower.
The clippers have vanished, but the yacht survives
as evidence of our ingenious conquest of the four
unpredictable winds. She's lovely as a nymph of Neptune.
Not all the iron afloat can ever supersede the dainty
racing sloop . . . while the wind blows free.

Photograph by Laurence R. Lowry

FURIOUS RIDE

Six wild horses plunge from the chutes, a three-man
team dragging on the rope halter of each.
It's the Wild Horse Race, a rare, dangerous rodeo event.
First you wrestle the bronc to the ground.
Next you saddle him, mount while he's down, and
get him to his feet. Then your teammates jump clear.
Their part is over—you ride the critter.
He bucks, whirls and sunfishes—rears up so far the sun

shines on his belly—and you've got 200 yards to go. If you make it to the finish line, you unsaddle and race to the judge in your high-heeled boots. If you're first, you win top money: sixty dollars. You split that three ways—a double sawbuck to each teammate. No event on the circuit causes more gasps than the Wild Horse Race, which helped draw this sellout crowd of 12,500 to the state championship rodeo in Sidney, Iowa, in August, 1955. Three men in the group above had broken arms when the race was over. Another, Johnny Hastings, the red-shirted boy in the middle with his arms outstretched, made it to the finish line, but hung one foot in the stirrup when he dismounted. The horse dragged him twenty feet and broke unlucky Johnny's leg.

Photograph by F. S. Nelson

THE LAND OF DANCING WATERS

The outflow of Swiftcurrent Lake drops 100 feet
in its short passage to Lake Sherburne. It tumbles
down the east slope of the Continental Divide
in the glacier country of Northwestern Montana.
Here two nations rule a primitive preserve
of Rocky Mountain alp and ice, lake and forest.
Forty-seven years ago the United States Congress
established Glacier National Park.
In 1932, Canada's Parliament added a piece of
Alberta Province to form Waterton-Glacier
International Peace Park. You may step across the
park's twenty-three-mile-long international
boundary without knowing it: no mine fields,
no barbed wire. Civilization has intruded
in the form of three hotels, a highway traversing
the Divide, guest chalets and truck trails.
But if a Blackfoot brave returned he would find
things largely unchanged off trail—plenty of
bighorn, elk, mule deer and beaver. And fish—
cutthroat, rainbow and brook trout, wary
but greedy, swift to strike and fight. Here on
Swiftcurrent water, John Mach, of Minneapolis,
uses the civilized fisherman's technique—
subtle, delicate and entrancing.

Photograph by Harland Sutherland—Kabel Photos   61

HERE LIVED A HERO

Next after God and country, he loved home and family.
The irony was that he was called away so much.
Young Washington had sixteen years at Mount Vernon
after he married Dan Custis's pretty widow, then it was
to horse, to arms and off to the wars again—for eight years.
Afterward he put a high-columned piazza on his
beloved mansion house, facing the Potomac, added a
banquet hall. Those were the years of "domestick ease
and happiness"—8000 acres to keep in order, foxes
to chase which usually got away. "Catch'd nothing,"
his diary said. Then the new nation required a President
and another eight years of his life. The last three
were his own. He died in his huge bed—he was a huge
man—at Mount Vernon. "I am not afraid to go,"
he remarked. He spent half his life serving his country.
His house is a noble shrine to one of the noblest Americans.

Photography by Ivan Dmitri

WHISTLE STOP

Sometimes the fast freight pauses for orders
at this way station in Hidalgo County,
New Mexico. The event is a welcome diversion
in a lonely land. This is Steins Stand, once
a stagecoach stop on the old Butterfield Trail
from Missouri to California. It perches atop
the 4347-foot summit of the pass through
the Peloncillo Mountains. Here, when
New Mexico was still a territory, travelers
to the West had one for the road before
descending through Doubtful Canyon where
Geronimo's murderous Apaches lurked.
For some, Steins was the Last Town on Earth.
But in September, 1880, Southern Pacific
track gangs, pushing eastward from Arizona,
made the Butterfield Trail obsolete.
Steam engines put the stagecoach drivers
out of work and soon the Apaches were
left unemployed too. Steins became a
whistle stop—population 45—where the
ghosts of whisky-breathing whipcrackers
and redskins prowl. Also the ghost of the Army
paymaster, who was murdered near Steins.
The Army found the corpse, but not the
payroll (it was in gold). The paymaster
evidently buried it before the Indians
killed him. Maybe it's out there in the hills
somewhere. Just where, nobody knows.

64   *Photograph by Bill Shrout*

COLOSSAL CLOWN

Jimmy the hippo lives a slovenly
happy life at America's oldest zoo,
in Philadelphia. A good-natured buffoon,
he wallows in an outsize puddle all day.
He can imitate a submarine or a whale,
a Teddy bear or a tank. He begs
for titbits as winsomely as a lap dog,
daintily accepting trifles in his huge maw.
He would make an invaluable tackle:
he weighs nearly three tons and,
when he wants to, can cover ground
with amazing speed. He is a cousin of the
common pig. Jimmy recently
became a father. Marie, the mistress
of his household, produced a fifty-pound
infant after a mere eight-month pregnancy.
For many weeks before the lying-in,
Jimmy was banished from the pool
he shared with Marie—he got
on her nerves. The baby, a boy hippo,
was named Limpopo. Jimmy took
his exile philosophically. The weather
was mild outside, and he knew that
a male around the house is superfluous
at birthings. Besides, life at the zoo is never
a bore. There are always chattering
crowds of human beings gathered around.
Jimmy seems to find them amusing.

Photograph by Gus Pasquarella   67

FAVORED VALLEY

In ages past, many men have gazed over the
Connecticut River Valley's rich earth, dreaming
of peace and plenty. First, as we know it, were
the copper-skinned Pocumtucs, who grew their corn,
pumpkins and tobacco and called their land Quinatucquet,
meaning "upon the long river." To this particular
scene, looking toward Mount Toby in Western
Massachusetts, came English settlers in 1672
to establish farms and villages. But they had to fight

to hold their prize and, before long, this frontier became a battleground — in thirty years of war with the Indians and the French. Near here occurred the Bloody Brook Massacre of 1675 and the great Deerfield Raid of 1704. Since then it has been a quiet land, mainly notable for fine tobacco. The first American "seegars" originated in the valley when farm wives rolled tobacco leaves into "Long Nines" and peddled them for pin money.

Today this soil produces the world's costliest tobacco, pampered and protected from sun, wind, and insects by vast cloth "shades," like those at lower left, which cover entire fields. It costs about $700 an acre to furnish this tentage. But shaded leaf is tender, smooth and light, and is worth $5 a pound as cigar wrappers. Such is the aristocratic descendant of the stringy, acrid weed that used to fill Pocumtuc peace pipes.

Photograph by A. H. Scott

A CITY'S GARDEN

Hard by Boston Common
lies the Public Garden, with its pond
where placid Swan Boats glide.
Robert Paget was licensed to operate the
boats three generations ago, and a
Paget still owns the concession.
A ride costs fifteen cents (children ten cents).
Brahmins and Gaels alike have loved
the Public Garden for a century—
since Boston's Back Bay was filled in,
about the time Ralph Waldo Emerson finally
concluded that slavery had to go.
Thereafter, with waves of Irish immigrants,
the Puritan city grew more robust and
rollicking. But the stamp of her
transcendental past still prevails in
Boston parks "bound in by streams which give
and take their colors from the sky."

70   *Photograph by Arthur Griffin*

IN SILENT MAJESTY

When these trees were young, a Pharaoh sat
on the throne of Thebes, and the druids practiced
their barbarous rites in what was to become
Shakespeare's Forest of Arden. Northern California's
redwoods are among the oldest and largest
living things, some of them well over 300 feet tall.
In age and weight, they yield only to their
brothers the Bigtrees—*Sequoia gigantea*. Botanists
call the redwoods *sempervirens*—ever-living.
Their recuperative powers are astonishing, as
attested by black scars on their trunks . . . scars
left by forest fires that burned unchecked
long before Columbus discovered America.
Once the redwoods were plundered for lumber.
But foresighted Californians appealed to Caesar to
spare the ancient gladiators. Since 1890, many stands
have been set aside in national parks and forests.
The trees shown are in the Humboldt tract
along the Redwood Highway, where
any citizen may picnic in a cathedrallike grove.
The trees survived nature's worst, and have
a good chance of escaping man's.
None has yet been known to die of old age.

72   *Photograph by Preston Duncan*

PRIZE BABIES

Competition begins early for youthful citizens of Circleville, Ohio, at the annual baby parade. Egged on by their eager elders, the diaper set trundles down Main Street in bonnets and bows, and the crowd coos. The judges are on a spot: They have to choose the best baby

right in the presence of the parents. The babies
are in none too comfortable a position, either, what
with the staring of the spectators and the starchiness
of the formal frocks. For the most part, however,
the brave little contestants carry on with
resigned composure: *noblesse oblige.*

To the winner, great honor, and a small prize:
Two dollars and fifty cents. Only one entry was truly
disillusioned in this contest held some months ago.
The infant in the upholstered carriage (lower right) decided
that, at those prices, he did not choose to compete.

Photograph by Ivan Dmitri

75

KENTUCKY HOME

Abe Lincoln was a peaceable man.
All his life he kept in his gentle heart a green
memory of Knob Creek farm in Kentucky,
where he lived as a little boy. Here, in a place
of "peace and grandeur, rocky cliffs, noble
trees and clear streams," he learned to read,
write and cipher to the rule of three.
His mother, Nancy, who died so young, still lived.
Does some aura of a seven-year-old Lincoln
linger here? The carefree, laughing spirit
of an unknown wilderness child who knows
nothing of the tragic future? Some say so,
and that's a happy thing to believe. The child
grew older and followed a hard road — to the west,
to the frontier in Illinois, to the White House,
to victory, sorrow and martyrdom.
In the great Lincoln Memorial at Washington,
we sense the greatness of his soul.
At Knob Creek, we sense the puckish genius
of woodland merriment that never left him.

Photograph by Frank Ross   77

SUNSET POINT

Tourists first saw California's Monterey Peninsula
over four hundred years ago. Did they look upon
Sunset Point—one of America's most photographed views?
No one knows. It is certain that the benign climate
seduced them—from the Spaniard Sebastián Vizcíano
to the American Bing Crosby, who golfs at Pebble Beach.

Adventurers and troubadours came. So did Padre Junípero, to win souls. He still lies in the mission at Carmel, a peninsula town. Between Carmel and Monterey, the coast is a privately operated park. The hidalgos of Old Mexico, whose California capital was Monterey, would find the cypress trees still undisturbed. Gold, in 1848, drew the promoters north from Monterey to San Francisco— fortunately for the peninsula of the conquistadores. Robert Louis Stevenson said here, "The finest meeting place of land and water in existence."

Photograph by Ivan Dmitri

79

MOSQUE
ON EMBASSY ROW

From the lacy stone heights of the minaret
floats the haunting call of the muezzin:
Allahu akbar . . . Ashhadu an la ilaha illa-llah—
"I testify there is no God but Allah."
The scene is not on the Nile, the Tigris or the
Golden Horn but on Massachusetts Avenue, N. W.,
Washington, D. C., and the chant is broadcast
by loud-speaker over the roar of traffic.
Twelve Eastern nations have built this magnificent
Islamic Center as a place of learning and
worship. Students of Moslem art and culture,
whatever their faith, are welcome in the
classrooms, library and museum, where they may
study Arabic or verses of the Koran.
The mosque itself sits at an angle, facing Mecca.
Here, in an atmosphere of pink Egyptian marble,
Turkish tile, ivory-inlaid wood and
hand-loomed Persian rugs, the faithful
followers of the Prophet Mohammed gather
when they hear the summons:
Hayya 'ala 's-Sala . . . Hayya 'ala 'l-Falah—
"Come to Prayer. . . . Come to Prosperity."

Photograph by Alfred Wagg

OLD SWIMMING HOLE

Everyone who ever lived in the country knows those
stifling summer days when the whole world droops
to a standstill. You *could* move (you tell yourself),
but it's just too hot. Then distant laughter
drifts up from the old swimming hole. You plunge
into whatever you were going to do, prompted
by the realization that you, too, can beat the heat.
Memories come back: The soft water
crawling into your nostrils as gently as a cat crawling
into your lap, dank coolness under the bank,
sand and weeds squirming underfoot, the girl whose
slight figure will always stay girlish in your mind.
These Alabama children are enjoying themselves in
picturesque Alligator Bayou, near Mobile,
but the happy mixture of youngsters and water
is everywhere, forever. For if there is a Fountain
of Youth, it is the old swimming hole with its
perennial invitation, "Come on in, the water's fine!"

82   *Photograph by Bill Shrout*

FISHERMAN'S WHARF

As befits a lady with a lot of history, Monterey's early record was one of continuous exploitation, but she was a glamour girl. In 1775, by royal Spanish decree, she was handsomely set up as the capital of colonial California. The revolutionary Mexican republic grabbed her from Spain in 1822 and kept her as its glamorous capital. (On the other hand, in 1818,

a French pirate named Bouchard sacked Monterey
and left without even tipping his beret.)
The hated Yankee exploiters finally cooked her goose,
transferring her franchise to Sacramento. She has
been fishing for a living ever since, and taking life easy.
At high noon of a pleasant day, Monterey's
Old Fisherman's Wharf dozes. Later in the afternoon

foot-loose townspeople and tourists will eat
at the wharf's fish bars. The air will be rent by the
panhandling screams of terns, sea gulls and pelicans.
And two mendicant sea lions from nearby Seal Island
off Point Lobos will show up to perform
slow-rolling acrobatics in return for fish scraps.

Photograph by Fred Ragsdale   85

OASIS
IN MANHATTAN

Sunday afternoon in New York may mean
cocktails on a penthouse terrace or gossip with
neighbors on the tenement's front steps.
It can also mean adventure in the far reaches
of the park. This 840-acre domain sees
many faces of the city: Along the eastern edge,
luxurious apartments and private houses
proceed northward in stately elegance.
Ultimately they yield to jam-packed slums.
The western side lies between a coliseum
rivaling Rome's, and the world's largest
Gothic cathedral. To the south loom
Manhattan's mightiest skyscrapers; to the
north stands Harlem. Within these disparate
bounds stretches a vast terrain of glade
and copse, lake and mere and rocky cliff. Here,
where New Yorkers' goats and pigs used to forage,
sprawls the city's celebrated big front yard.
A girl can sit barefoot on sun-splashed rocks
and bring her Sunday paper to read
where once Manahata savages roamed.
The Indians sold this land to the white invader
for a bargain price, and soon—
in the early nineteenth century—
real-estate values inflated enormously.
It took the city ten years to find the money
to buy the land for this natural preserve.
Fortunately, farsighted men won out,
and New York acquired the wonderful wilderness
of Central Park, one hundred years ago.

Photograph by George Tichenor   87

AMERICAN
INHERITANCE

Here repose the three most
precious documents in the U.S.A.
In the upright case with bronze doors is
the Declaration of Independence. Below it are
the Constitution and the Bill of Rights.
Half a million persons a year
file past these venerable parchments by day;
each night an ingenious mechanism
lowers the unit containing them into a vault
twenty feet below the floor of the National
Archives Exhibition Hall in Washington.
Not always have these documents
rested so securely, nor in such dignity.
When the British sacked the capital in 1814,
the three great charters,
stuffed in coarse linen sacks,
were conveyed to safety in Virginia.
More recently, in World War II,
they were deposited variously
in Fort Knox and in another secret stronghold.
But until danger threatens again,
they remain in plain view,
a reminder that rights hard won need
eternal vigilance lest they be irretrievably lost.

88 *Photograph by George and Jim Burns*

DUNE DENIZENS

You see here some members of one of America's
First Families, spirited creatures which might belong
to a sort of Society of Mayflower Descendants if horses
had such things. Their ancestors arrived in the early 1700's
when their ship was wrecked on Ocracoke Island,

a North Carolina sandspit near treacherous
Cape Hatteras. Since then the horses have run loose.
They are rounded up annually, and new colts
are branded by the owners of the wild mares which bore
them. To thin out the herd Ocracoke holds an auction
each Fourth of July. The horses bring $50 to $100 each,
after which the buyer must pay for ferrying them
thirty miles to the nearest railhead. But Ocracoke retains
enough to supply mounts for its Boy Scout troop.

Photograph by George Tichenor

UNEXPECTED LAKE

Nature built some of her most fabulous scenery
in the high Rockies of Southwestern Colorado.
And mighty adventurers left footprints and
fanciful names in these mountains: To westward
lie the Rio Dolores — River of Sorrows —
and its tributary, the Disappointment.
The peaks in the background are named for the
Archangel Michael. The people in the foreground
are two miles east of Lizard Head Pass,
six miles south of Ilium, four miles west of Ophir.
This little lake, called Trout Lake,
a two-mile-high surprise to the traveler in these
unfrequented parts, provides rich sport for anglers.
It is actually a hydroelectric power reservoir.
Who lives here? A few vacationists,
in the summer; but in the winter no one but
Byron Brown and his wife. He tends
the dam machinery in the buildings at left for
the Western Colorado Power Company.
Do the Browns ever get cabin fever
from the lonely life? It's too soon to tell.
One of Byron's predecessors, Tom Jennings,
lived here alone for fifty years, and he liked it fine.

Photograph by Jack Breed

THE COOL COAST

If you straightened out the shore line of Maine
it would reach from Portland to Panama,
for the great ice age left thousands of harbors
and hideaways between Kittery and Passamaquoddy.
Shown here is a cove near Ogunquit, stretching
from Short Sands Beach (foreground) to Lobster Point,
which the beacon marks. Leif the Lucky probably
sailed past this ragged coast in his Viking ships
a thousand years ago. He was followed by a host
of Spaniards, Frenchmen and Englishmen.
Spanish interests lay elsewhere, but the French and
English turned Maine into a battleground and
generally raised hob over these parts for the best part
of a century. It was from such struggle and
hardship that the hardy down-East breed evolved.
State of Mainers today remain as ruggedly independent
as when they broke off from Massachusetts to form
a separate state. Yet, noting the lure that piny woods
and cool summer air have for denizens of
the sweaty cities, they have softened in their attitude
toward outlanders. Since the 1870's, part-time Mainers,
called cottagers—like the folk on these beaches—
have been one of the state's biggest businesses.
Indeed, every Maine automobile advertises
that Maine is Vacationland.

94   *Photograph by Frank Ross*

BIG BACK YARD

Beyond the burgeoning cities, Texas ranges roll in
gentle swells to the horizon and beyond, a fair,
oak-dotted grassland vaster than many nations are.
But if Mother Nature weren't meddled with a bit,
soon she would clothe this land in underbrush,
a hard-to-chew diet that cattle don't go for at all.
So to the rescue come Mr. Billy and Mrs. Nanny Goat,
and their relatives and friends; they dine blissfully on
young brush shoots, leaving room on the table
for the serving of grass and clover, called ambrosia
on a bovine menu. This is Aaron Alford's ranch
and that's his son-in-law, Curtis Caffey, beyond the
goat herd; Aaron grazes 100 head of cattle
in his 500-acre back yard, and George Bredt (left)
ranches where he isn't cramped for space, either,
far away where the sky dips low.
For a change, Aaron and his wife can run down to
metropolitan Austin, 91 miles away,
but why leave for long a spot where one can call
so much lovely elbowroom one's own?

Photograph by Bill Shrout

LIGHTSHIP

The world's most famous floating lighthouse
lies anchored eleven miles southeast of Coney Island.
She carries the brightest of all lightship lights
(more than 1,000,000 candlepower) and, in
foggy weather, bellows in a monstrous voice that
can be heard six miles away. Her name is Ambrose,
after the channel she marks. From her,
ships take their course into the port of New York,
and their departure for ports of all the world.
She is the first bit of America seen by countless visitors,
and the last bit of America seen by unlucky voyagers
who perish in the deeps. Great liners pass her
close aboard, as near as 100 yards, to take a good look.
Here the Queen of Bermuda, outbound on
a pleasure cruise, salutes her spunky little sister.
Today the sea is calm and bright.
But through furious storms when all other ships
run for cover, and through impenetrable fogs
when homing vessels sometimes even ram her,
Ambrose remains a prisoner of her chains.
One of her anchors lost its grip recently in a hurricane.
The seas rose to terrifying heights,
but the other anchor held and the light burned on.
Later the captain reported laconically on the storm.
"The Ambrose Lightship remained on station," he said.

Photograph by Maynard Clark

THE EARTH IS GOOD

The Dunkard farmers of York County, Pennsylvania,
are noted for their piety, and an abiding love of good,
tilled earth. Here in Dunkards' Valley, ten miles
south of the city of York, are fields tended by Dunkards
ever since the eighteenth century, when founders
of this sect of Baptists were harried out of Germany.
The farm is owned now by Emore Lehman.

SENTRY BY THE SEA

On a calm summer day West Quoddy Head Light,
southeast of Lubec, Maine, snoozes in the sun.
Its 10,000-candlepower lamp rests and the
foghorn's mighty voice is still. But lighthouses
along this rugged coastline seldom have a chance
to loaf like this, for thick fogs and 28-foot tides
keep them busy warning sailors from rocks and shoals.
Quoddy Light's greatest distinction is geographical:
It stands on the easternmost point in the United States.
Across the Lubec Channel lies Campobello,
a Canadian island which was Franklin D. Roosevelt's
summer home. On summer weekends,
tourists flock to West Quoddy Head, but the light's
biggest audience is composed of the fishermen
sailing home to Lubec, and the crews of coastal
cargo ships, yachts and passing deep-sea vessels.
It is for them that this gaudy sentry flashes
its friendly, characteristic signal—two seconds on,
two off, two on, nine off—a reassuring signpost
for anxious navigators on the trackless sea.

106   *Photograph by Arthur Griffin*

THE FACE OF
AMERICA
IN
AUTUMN

YANKEE AUTUMN

Now New England summer wanes.
Elms and maples flaunt brave colors before
submitting to the long White Mountain winter.
This is New Hampshire, a state of the Union
as long as there has been a Union.
Of the thirteen colonies, New Hampshire
first set up a government independent of the king.
So much for tyranny—and it was thriftier too.
Town meeting once a year—gets done what
needs doing. Here in Andover village, meeting
started in 1773. Forthright deeds, frugal words:
Speak your mind and sit down.
(Of course, a Yankee *can* speechify:
Daniel Webster could outtalk anyone. He was
a Salisbury man, born two miles from here.)
Three hundred people live in Andover,
with 120 boys of Proctor Academy, a young school:
New Hampshire's had schools for 300 years.
Proctor wasn't founded until 1848. The buildings
belong to Proctor, Slocomb Hall at right. Why does
the other look like a church? Used to be one.
Congregationalists gave it up. School bought it,
made an infirmary out of it. Waste not, want not.

Photograph by Harland Sutherland—Kabel Photos

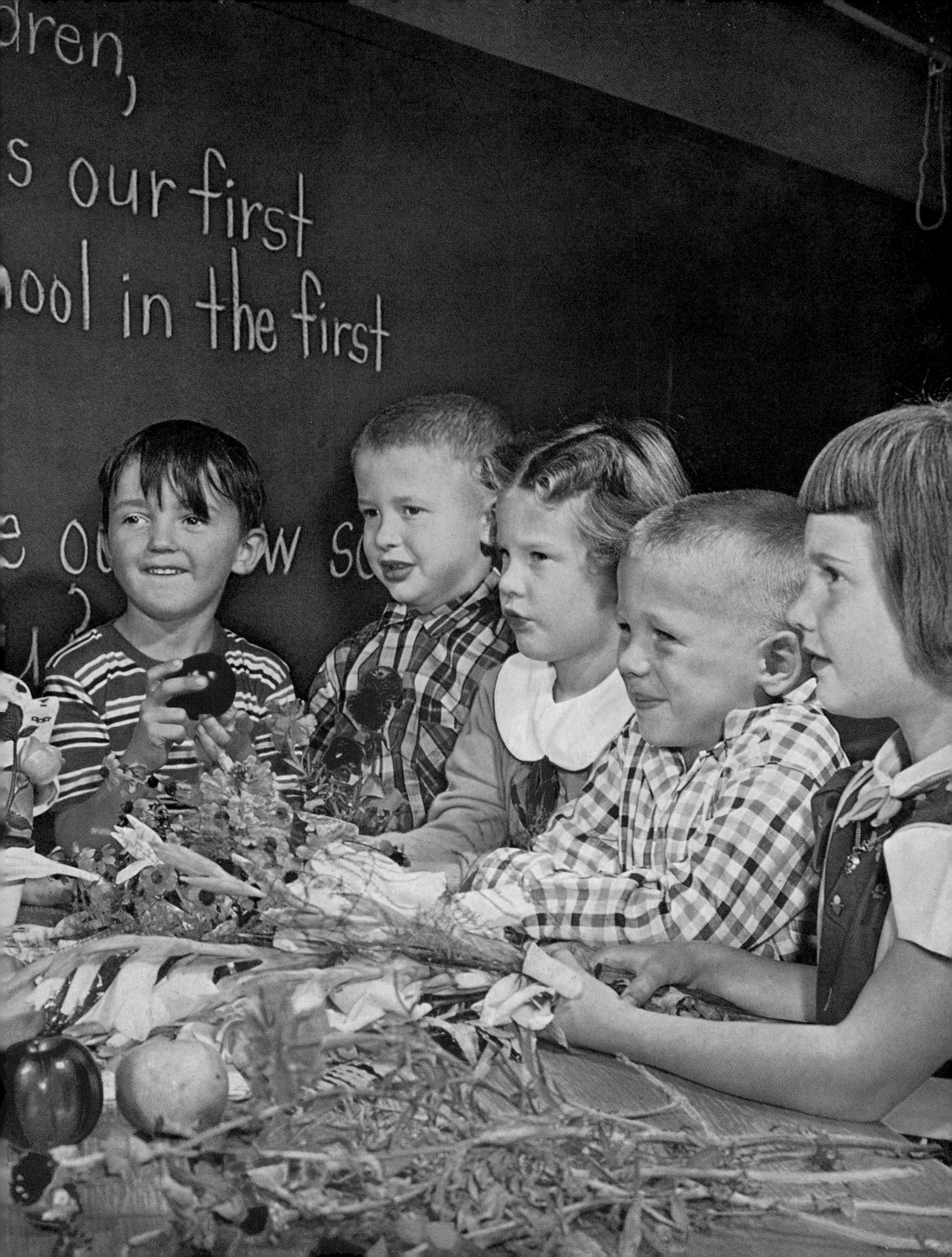
dren,
s our first
hool in the first

FIELD OF GOLD

Warren Anderson's Ohio farm lies south
of the Lincoln Highway, between Mansfield
and Massillon. He and his wife,
Anna, have brought up three daughters
and two sons on these 265 acres.
All the children are married now.
Since the boys left home, Warren tills only
seventy-five acres. He keeps Durham cattle—
to fatten and sell in Cleveland, others
for milk—and a flock of breeding ewes.
He crops corn, oats, hay and wheat.
"I keep some wheat in shock every year,"
he says. "I want the straw to bed the stock.
I like a straw pile in the barnyard."
So the shocks march in regimental ranks
across the stubbly field, the land lies golden
and still. The Andersons recall years of
fulfillment that this earth has given them.
But they think ahead to other springs, when the
wheat will rise again, young and green.

Photograph by Harland Sutherland—Kabel Photos

CITY OF SPLENDOR

Here, in evening clothes, glitters San Francisco,
the first great boom town of the Golden West,
birthplace of the U.N. and home of Joe DiMaggio.
Sir Francis Drake sighted the harbor in 1579,
but it took a gold rush to establish the city.
Jack London and Robert Louis Stevenson
roamed the notorious Barbary Coast,
and empire builders like Mark Hopkins and
"Bonanza Jim" Fair built gingerbread castles on
Nob Hill. The shimmering ribbons of traffic
at the center of this time exposure trail steeply
from that famous hill down California Street.
At far right is the Russ Building, tallest structure
in the city. The brightly lighted tower
on the Embarcadero tops the Ferry Building,
once the country's busiest transportation terminal.
Now most traffic rolls—or creeps—over the
double-decked eight-and-one-fourth-mile-long
San Francisco-Oakland Bay Bridge. Daniel Webster
said this bay alone was twenty times more
valuable than Texas. To hundreds of thousands of
servicemen home-bound from the Pacific,
San Francisco symbolized all America.
San Franciscans love their town, and though some
disparage its fog and steep hills, all agree
on one point: The name, please, is not "Frisco."

116   *Photograph by Glenn Embree*

CAMPUS PROCESSION

Eager youngsters are swarming to the campuses
in increasing numbers. There are some
2,800,000 collegians now; by 1960 there'll be over a
third of a million more. Colleges and universities
everywhere are struggling with the problems
of absorbing more students. Take 102-year-old
Cornell College, at Mount Vernon, Iowa.
Traditionally small, Cornell recently lifted its
enrollment from 600 to 750 and began hunting for funds.
They've got a new fieldhouse, a new
health center. The Olin Foundation donated
a 183-man dormitory, promised to pay for a
new library-social center too. The Ford Foundation
gave $211,000 to help boost teachers' salaries.
But foundations can't do the job alone.
Private citizens, parents of students, alumni have to help.
That's the situation at Cornell, the situation almost
everywhere. Shown here, the procession from
Cornell's King Memorial Chapel on Parents' Day
in October, 1955, when the new dorm—named
for gunpowder king F. W. Olin—was dedicated.

Photograph by Ivan Dmitri

DOWN EAST

For seven generations Maine men
have put ships to sea from their
fog-shrouded coast—some bearing
U.S. battle flags to troubled corners of
the world, others taking American
traders to the islands of Polynesia and
far Cathay. And all the while, from
coves and inlets along the serrated coast,
Yankee fishermen cruise the inexhaustible
storehouse of the North Atlantic,
each bringing home his share
of the sea's gifts. Many of their boats
and most of their gear are the same today
as they were a century and more ago.
The old broad-beamed smacks shown here
go to sea in fair weather and foul.
At the same time, diesel-powered
trawlers, equipped with radar and other
modern scientific devices adapted
from the Navy, ply their trade alongside
the old-timers. Maine men, it has
been said, are a mixture of orneriness,
wisdom and serenity. Slow to discard the
old ways, they are quick to exploit
the new ones. So for generations to come,
fishermen will work the down-East
coast in fog and gale, in boats not far
different from those used 2000 years ago.
Radar can see in the dark, to be
sure, but a Maine fisherman has
a sailor's sixth sense to guide him—
and in the long run, he considers it more
reliable than any electronic gadget.

Photograph by Bill Rapp   121

DEN MEETING

Cub Scouting means many things.
It means wearing the blue-and-gold uniform,
standing inspections, honoring the flag.
It's baseball and cook-outs and make-believe.
It's learning to tie a clove hitch, build a radio,
plant a garden. It's a chance for city boys
like these Chicago Cubs to study nature and
wildlife — here a fox (stuffed) is being analyzed
for young Cubs by Den Chief Danny Hall,
an eleven-year-old Boy Scout.
Listening in is the Den Mother,
Mrs. Raymond D. Hall, who in her
nonofficial capacity is the real mother of two of
these lads. The Cub Scout movement itself
is now full grown at age twenty-five
and includes one out of every four American
boys in the eight-to-ten age bracket.
They come in all shapes and sizes, colors
and creeds, but they all take the same pledge:
"I promise to do my best, to do my duty
to God and my country, to be square
and to obey the law of the pack."

Photograph by Frank Ross   123

CROSSROADS
OF HISTORY

Out of the darkness on an autumn night in 1859,
a self-appointed avenging angel descended
on this peaceful village. Here, at the gap
in the Blue Ridge Mountains in West Virginia,
where the Shenandoah joins the Potomac,
lies the town of Harpers Ferry. And here
Osawatomie John Brown, from the bloody plains
of Kansas, came to defy the Government
of the United States with his little army
of twenty-two men. He came to free all Negroes
from slavery, and the first man his force killed
was Heywood Shepherd, a free Negro.
Brown occupied the Armory, which stood
on the near shore of the Potomac, at left,
where only the rectangles of white stones mark
its site today. It took the U. S. Marines to dislodge
the fanatical old man. They hanged John Brown,
but soon the tides of war washed over Harpers Ferry.
Many more men died, singing of
John Brown's body amoldering in the grave,
before all Negroes were free. Now Harpers Ferry
drowses once more, a peaceful village again—
haunted only by dreams of the dark and tragic past.

Photograph by Maynard Clark 125

UNDER THE HIGH TETONS

From the plateau of Western Wyoming
these American Alps reach to the sky.
Here, some fifty years ago, T. A. Moulton
homesteaded on the last frontier.
And while wars were fought and atoms were split,
the unchanging mountain valley known as the
Jackson Hole Country yielded him a
hard-won living. "Raised a family of two boys
and four girls," he says. "Put 'em all
through high school, one through college."
Now, with a job well done behind him,
Moulton lets the two boys run the ranch.
In the long, bitter Wyoming winter—
sometimes it hits forty below—range alone cannot
support stock, so Moulton Ranch cattle must
be fed hay and grain throughout half of
every year. Here, with an old-time thresher
and a horse-drawn rig, Clark and Harley Moulton
harvest September oats, which they raise,
along with hay and barley, for feed.
In summer Old Man Moulton tastes the winy air
of the Rockies and gazes up to the awesome,
protective heights of the Grand Tetons.
"Jackson Hole has been good to me,"
he says. "Best place in the world."

Photograph by Grant Heilman   127

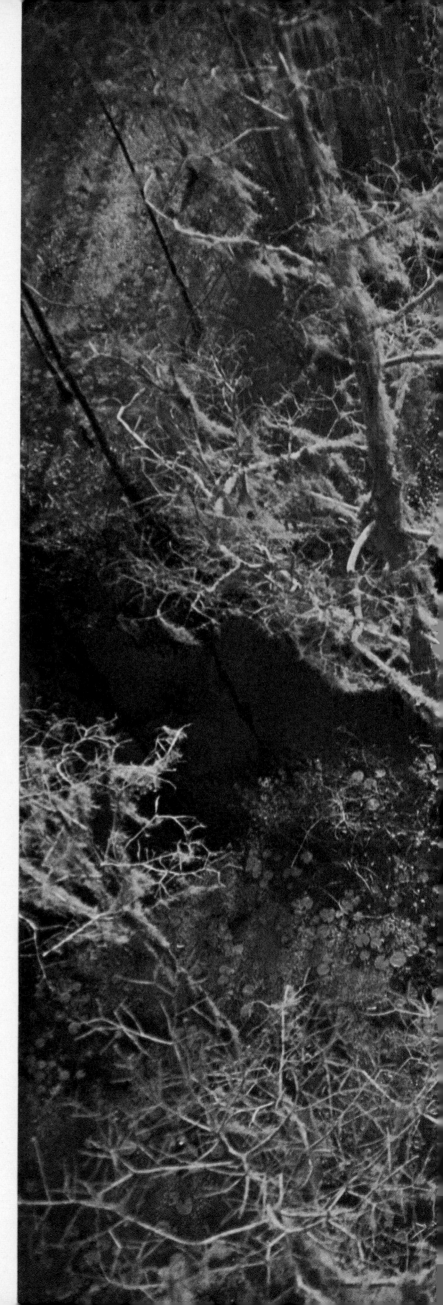

NICE SWAMP

Southerners usually swear *at* their swamps.
South Carolina's swampiest is called Hell Hole,
Virginia's biggest is Dismal.
But folks who know Okefenokee Swamp, in Georgia,
swear *by* the place. Finest swamp in the world, they say.
It drains itself. No stagnant water, few mosquitoes, and
the alligators and snakes hardly ever bite anybody.
Even the name has a pleasant sound,
like a patent medicine you could swallow.
That's because, like many patent-medicine names,
it is Indian. It means "trembling land."
Until halted by law, hunters slaughtered the
swamp gators for leather. Now swamp patrolmen,
such as the two you see here, scout for illicit gunners.
Okefenokee has two claims to fame,
thanks to people who never saw it.
Walt Kelly made it the home of his comic-strip
opossum, Pogo. Stephen Foster wrote a song
which has been sung a billion times about a river
that rises right here in the Okefenokee.
Its name: Suwannee.

Photograph by Robert E. Gerlach

JAM SESSION

An infernal racket to some, but a sublime pattern
of sound to others, hot jazz is America's
most distinctive contribution to music.
In each generation its freewheeling rhythm
attracts new devotees. They respond not with
the rapt silence of symphony audiences
but with the open exuberance of this crowd
listening to some solid sending by the Jive Bombers
at Charles Wade's Airport Inn in Troy, New York.
As at any concert, a few of the customers
obviously aren't with it; they are wondering
what other people see in this sort of stuff, anyway.
Jazz originally evolved during the scandalously
Gay Nineties in French-settled New Orleans,
where unschooled Negro musicians
applied their bounce and inventiveness
to the French popular tunes of the day.
Jazz moved after World War I to Chicago
and spread over the land and across the Atlantic,
being hailed by some of the most high-domed
European intellectuals as a new creative art form.
Its flavor has been the basic ingredient in
the success of some of the biggest dance bands,
under jazzmen such as Benny Goodman and
the Dorsey brothers and Glenn Miller.
However, the most down-to-earth jazz
generally comes out of "jam sessions"
by small groups like this four-piece combo:
Clarence Palmer, bass; Earl Johnson, sax;
Pee-Wee Tinney, drums; Al Tinney, piano.

Photograph by Jim Burns

can outpull all others of equal size. For more than a century contests to settle such questions have been—and still are—popular features at county fairs. The rules are fairly simple: A call booms out, "Hustle those cattle in here, you drivers," and the crowds gather at the pulling ring.
Here, at the West Oxford Fair, Fryeburg, they

are watching Star and Line, owned by Roger Bragdon, of North Berwick, win a distance class by pulling a boat loaded with 2000 pounds of stone 126 feet, nine inches, in five minutes. Winners get local glory, little cash; Bragdon's purse was $6.50.

Photograph by Kosti Ruohomaa   141

SUNDOWN

Some years ago, the Lee Brooks family
and their horse, Sundown, moved from New York
to California and founded Sundown Ranch.
There they raise dogs and horses on a
180-acre tract in Slaughterhouse Canyon, a
peacefully remote suburb of Hollywood.
Brooks horses have thundered through many a
Hollywood Western, and one of their dogs rubbed noses
with a flying saucer in a science-fiction thriller. But
the family's principal business is breeding Shetland ponies
and training horses and dogs for private owners.
Sundown, their amazing palomino stallion,
loves to play ball and can retrieve as expertly
as a trained dog. He is retired to pasture now,
where he keeps a proud eye on one of his offspring,
called Little Sundown. What finer place
for horse—or human being—to retire?
The climate in this colorful country
is "typical of Southern California," says Mrs. Brooks,
"without the smog." Which is a real blessing
particularly during these serene moments when shadows
begin to dance over the sagebrush hills—at sundown.

142

Photograph by Art Riley

AUTUMN MAGIC

The sorcerer waves his wand, changing colors
at will, bringing the great illusion to a
flaming climax. The haunting wind music mutes
before the final crescendo, as the last performance
of the season draws to a close.
Soon the curtain will fall, and the theater
of all outdoors—cold, drafty and draped in white—
will stand empty for next spring's opening.
Here in New England the first thin watery snowfall
signals a warning, and the maple leaves of
Sugar Hill, New Hampshire, in colorful costume still,
hasten to make their exit, fluttering off stage
as gracefully as ballerinas. The sorcerer bows,
folds his dark cloak about him and departs.
Icy winter has no pity for mountebanks such as he,
and his next show doesn't begin until April.

Photograph by Arthur Griffin 145

THE FACE OF
AMERICA
IN
WINTER

TREE OF ICE

Winter is quick to seize the northern Great Plains
in his inexorable grip. Soon after the rich Dakota wheat
has been harvested the ground hardens,
and trees in the windbreaks stiffen.
The people take to the snug comforts of their homes;
stinging, snow-filled gales swirl unchecked across
the frozen land, and months of unbroken cold follow.
Yet sometimes during this long, numbing
season Winter makes a special effort to
redeem himself for the bleak visitation. Here on
Sebastian Young's farm near Harvey, North Dakota,
you witness one of these rare moments.
Earlier on this Sunday morning a heavy fog had
lain over his 730 acres of table-flat land.
The temperature—a brittle, crackling eighteen
below zero—had been, in Farmer Young's words,
"a little above average" for mid-January.
Then an emboldened sun burned through the
opaque white blanket, and turned the sky
to a brilliant blue. And there on the trees in the
foreground Winter had worked his most delicate magic:
a crystalline fretwork of ice encasing the
willow branches, preserving the silent vapors
of the night in the curious transmutation of frozen fog.

Photograph by Ivan Dmitri   149

WINTER PLAYGROUND

There are anywhere from a half million
to three and a half million skiers in this country,
depending on whether you count only those
fanatics who hit the slopes every winter weekend,
or include the others who manage to put on
their boards only once or twice a year.
They range in age from toddlers
(note the pickaback skier) to septuagenarians,
and they all claim it's the greatest sport on earth.
Skiing didn't make much headway in the United States
until the late '30's, when the introduction of ski lifts
made it possible to zip down a mountain
without spending several hours climbing back up.
Since then, everything from rope tows to
alpine lifts has been built on hillsides and mountains;
thousands of rural communities have found
that there's gold in them thar hills—
carried in by skiers. This is the lodge at Alta, Utah—
one of the most famous ski areas in the country,
where skiers find knee-deep powder snow
from Thanksgiving to May.

Photograph by Frank Ross

DAIRY FARM IN VERMONT

On clear winter days, rural Vermont stands forth
in Yankee Doodle colors, with red barns,
white snow and blue skies. The scene is typical
in a state of 20,000 farms, snow-clad from December
until mid-March. Draft horses are still valued here.
This team is driven by Stephen C. Cooke, on his dairy farm
at Bridport, in the Lake Champlain Valley.

Here he spreads fertilizer, as he does almost
every winter's day, against the time of spring seeding.
Horses can pull the spreader through depths of snow that
bring his tractors to a standstill. In other respects,
Mr. Cooke's farm is thoroughly mechanized, as it must be.
His milk shipments average a ton a day the year round;
Boston gets it all. To keep up this production,

Mr. Cooke manages a herd of 225 cattle,
and a 600-acre spread of pasture and cropland.
His annual harvest runs to 700 tons of corn
and 35,000 bales of hay. Good land, this, and a credit
to generations of Cookes. They've owned it,
father and son, for more than a hundred and fifty years.

Photograph by Frank Ross   153

TUGBOATS OF TACOMA

In the northwest corner of the U.S.A.
the Pacific extends a watery arm—Puget Sound—
into the state of Washington. Here lie great
bustling seaports and dozens of lesser cities,
all connected by hundreds of miles of waterway.
This is the native habitat of Tugboat Annie.
Without tugboats, the industry of this
Puget Sound city, Tacoma, would be crippled.
At lower right, the powerful little tug, Joe Foss,
hauls a boom of logs uptide to a sawmill.
Astern of the Joe Foss, another tug, the Brynn Foss,
pushes a bargeload of sawdust against the pier.
The sawdust, waste from Puget Sound mills,
will go into the enormous heap dominating
the center of the picture. That's the city's woodpile,
fuel for the furnaces that heat much
of downtown Tacoma via a central system.
The pile shown will just about last through the winter.
Next summer, with the tugs still hard at work,
it will grow again. Inspired, perhaps,
by the mighty height of Mount Rainier—
the snowy peak in the background—
the tugboats of Tacoma never stop trying to build
the biggest pile of sawdust in the world.

Photograph by John Bickel   155

QUEEN
OF THE CAMPUS

During Pageant Week at the State University of Iowa
the prettiest girls compete for the crown of Miss SUI.
A would-be queen must visit fraternity houses
with an ensemble of her sisters in support.
Carole Bartels, for example—at the
Alpha Epsilon Pi house in the small picture above—
brought along a chorus line in fur-trimmed bathing suits,
to do an uninhibited number called Honey Bun
(thunderous applause). Dorothy Nakano, of Hawaii,
did a hula (enthusiastic shouts). Ertzie Kerns presented
a quintet in leotards (appreciative whistles).
Most competitors let their teams do the plugging,
but Dora Lee Martin, a 17-year-old freshman
from Houston, Texas, starred in her own act,
singing The Yellow Rose of Texas (ovation).
On Friday, December 9, 1955, the male students cast
1924 ballots. On Saturday at the gala winter dance,
the queen was crowned: Dora Lee, winner by fifty votes.
This was big news because Dora Lee is a Negro,
the only one in a field of twenty-nine candidates,
and one of only 150 Negroes among SUI's 9000 students.
The story was on the wires immediately,
and most of Iowa City learned of
Dora Lee's triumph later than New York City.

Photographs by Ivan Dmitri   157

MORMON TEMPLE

Heavenly personages, Mormons believe, appeared to
Joseph Smith, an obscure Yankee boy, in the 1820's.
Thus was born the Church of Jesus Christ
of Latter-day Saints. Years of turmoil followed.
Smith never saw the Promised Land he envisioned—
he died at the hands of a mob.
Indomitable Brigham Young led the Saints
to a fertile Utah valley and said, "This is the place!"
Now Salt Lake City stands
a monument to persistence. In its midst lies
the elliptical-roofed Tabernacle, and the great
Temple which no non-Mormon may enter.
In the Tabernacle (lower left in the photograph)
worldly affairs are debated. In the brilliantly lighted
Temple sacred ceremonies are celebrated.
A stouthearted Christian people, Mormons claim
"the privilege of worshiping Almighty God
according to the dictates of our own conscience,
and allow all men the same. . . ."

158   *Photograph by Frank Ross*

WINTER FISHING CAMP

Up in the nervous North, from Seattle to Chicago
to Manhattan, cold rains drip and December
winds moan through the cities' concrete canyons.
But down below the thirtieth parallel
on the river called the Dead, subtropical breezes
ripple placid waters where black bass lurk.

Here rich idlers and poor philosophers enjoy perpetual summer amidst flowers that never cease to bloom. The Dead River, which is only about a mile long, connects two lakes. At the northern end of this two-headed stream, where Highway 441 crosses it, sits this cottage, one of dozens of fishing camps in watery Lake County. Florida has many faces: Some busy, some gay, some glamorous, some raucous. But here in her midlands are secret gardens where an angler can fish in peace, far from glittering night clubs and restless pari-mutuel machines.

Photograph by A. H. Scott

161

COPS AND KIDS

Bicycles, like automobiles, are only as safe as their drivers.
Policemen in Upper Darby, Pennsylvania,
make sure their town's boys and girls acquire
safe cycling habits from the day they take to the open road.
As part of a safety program, the kids must get driving licenses
as soon as they get bikes.
License No. 1 went out in 1954 to twelve-year-old
Mary Ellen Boyle, daughter of the police superintendent.
Since then, thousands of cyclists have qualified.
The.tags and registration cards are free.
The costs of the program are borne by the local Optimist Club.
Here, at the testing course in Naylor's Run Park,
Sgt. Mike Laub (foreground) and fellow officers put
a group of school children through their paces.
The test includes an inspection, driving test and oral quiz on
traffic regulations. Kids and cops get a big kick out of
the program, but there's a deadly serious purpose behind it.
In a typical year, 500 Americans die
and 44,000 are injured in bicycle accidents.

Photograph by Gus Pasquarella   163

MOMENT IN WINTER

Streams are not always beautiful, but in the country
they are rarely ugly, and they have many
moments of exaltation, most of which are unseen
by man. Sometimes they even experience
fleeting glows of transfiguration. Here you see
such a glow in a branch of the Green River
as it passes through rural South Williamstown in
the northwest corner of Massachusetts.
Late in the afternoon of an overcast day,
while the branch was running blackly between
immaculate borders of snow, a falling sun
broke cloud. Briefly, it painted the water a blood-red
as if to remind the world of the fruitfulness
that awaited birth beneath the drifts.
The mood lasted only a minute or so.
A perceptive photographer, heading for an
assignment further on, saw it, stopped
his car on a little bridge, unlimbered a camera
and shot quickly. Then he got back into
his car and drove on in the gathering dusk,
hoping that his hastily set camera controls had
been right and that he had impaled a
rare moment of beauty on his film. He had.

164   *Photograph by Ivan Dmitri*

DUCKS' WINTER RESORT

Deep in the ever-changing lower delta of the Mississippi,
watercourses wind between cut-grass and willows.
This is the land of the "trembling prairie,"
where all travel is afloat. The waters abound with fish,
and here are wintering grounds of northern wildfowl,
the terminus of the flyway from Canada.
The lower delta has passes, as a mountain range has.
Ellis Loga and his son Cleve are setting out decoys
in Dennis Pass, an offshoot of Pass à Loutre.
All Louisiana once was part of Napoleon's Empire.
Immutable Gaul survives in delta names, faces and speech.
Loga works for the state. He keeps a clubhouse in
public game lands—fifteen miles by water from Venice,
a delta town. He is helped by Cleve, by his brother Benny
and by the dog, whose name is Book. A century and
a half ago the lower delta was the domain
of the sea rovers, like Jean Lafitte and Nez Coupé.
The Spanish Main supports pirates no more,
but buccaneers' descendants still dwell in the deep delta.
They're law-abiding, but piratically independent and carefree.
They inherited corsair blood—and they're proud of it.

166   *Photograph by Bill Shrout*

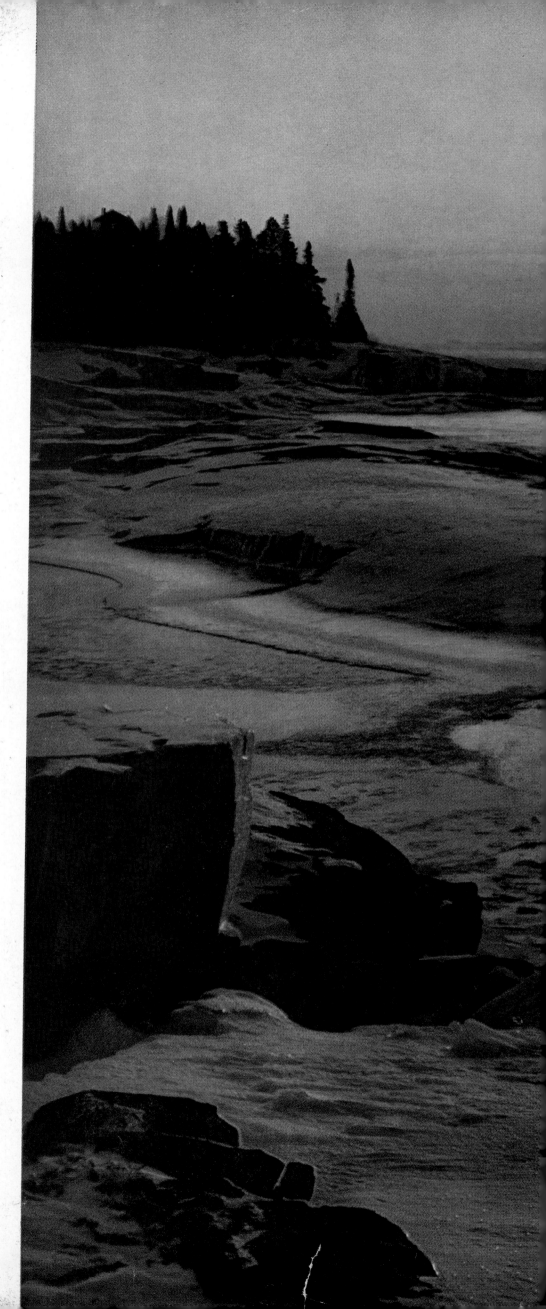

FROZEN SUNRISE

Winter comes early to Northern Minnesota, and cold bites deep into the land. On this morning, the air is a crackling ten degrees below zero, as a weak sun rises out of Lake Superior to strike sudden color from the ice-sheathed shore near Grand Marais. This is old Chippewa country, opened up in the mid-1600's by trappers and fur traders—first French, then British, finally American. Long gone now, these hardy men left their mark in the place names they gave.

North from Grand Marais—in French, Big Marsh—the old Gunflint Trail still winds toward nearby Canada into a region studded with lakes called Devil's Track, East Bearskin and Hungry Jack. Some say these lakes were gouged from a younger earth by the glacial ice; lumbermen will tell you they are the footprints of Paul Bunyan.

Today tourists have replaced the trappers, and the old trading posts have given way to vacation cabins and lodges, but the past still seems very close, and the wilderness has changed remarkably little since Bunyan passed this way.

Photograph by Thomas Peters Lake

CHURCH

The old town church of Peterborough, New Hampshire,
has a brand-new preacher: Here young David Boynton Parke is ordained
and installed as the twenty-fourth minister in a line stretching back to 1752.
The Rev. Mr. Parke and his congregation are Unitarians—that is,
they believe in the oneness of Christian fellowship and of God,
but subscribe to no creeds. Mr. Parke has always been a Unitarian,
but the church was originally Presbyterian and later Congregational.
It became Unitarian only at about the time the present edifice (below)
was built, in 1825, from designs by the celebrated Charles Bulfinch.
David Parke visited Peterborough in 1947, when he was only eighteen.
His ambition to serve the historic church was born then.
Nine years later, a young husband and father freshly graduated from
theological school at the University of Chicago, he found the
Peterborough incumbency vacant, applied for the job and got it.
Now, at twenty-seven, he assumes responsibility for the spiritual needs
of 170 townspeople. The lay "president" of the church, Richard C. Johnson,
places the gown of office on David's shoulders, and the young man
inherits the tradition of Adams, Longfellow, Emerson, Hawthorne,
Holmes, Louisa M. Alcott and all the generations of Yankees
who hold to their right to worship in their own independent way.

Photographs by Larry Keighley

SUGARING-OFF

The sugar maple is a versatile tree:
Well formed and often more than 100 feet tall,
it lends elegance to park and avenue. In autumn
it stuns the eye with theatrical coloration.
Its light-colored, close-grained wood is excellent
for furniture and flooring. As a fuel it is
slow-burning, hot and pleasantly aromatic.
And, in early spring, it yields a thin,
sweetish sap which can be boiled down to produce
syrup or sugar—as memorable a sweetening
as you'll find anywhere in the world.
The American Indians introduced maple sugar
to the pioneers of Canada and New England.
Now there are seven million trees
in the eleven states of Vermont, New York,
Pennsylvania, Michigan, Ohio, New Hampshire,
Wisconsin, Massachusetts, Maine, Maryland
and Minnesota producing over 150,000 pounds of
sugar and a million and a half gallons of syrup
annually. Here we see farmer Walter H. Tower,
of Worthington, Mass., collecting sap from the
fifteen acres he reserves for maple-sugar production.
After 55 years in the business he still believes
that a horse and sled is the best way to get around
when the snow lies deep in the maple forests.

Photograph by Carl Howard   173

SONG OF OLD

Silent in the twilight lies the mountain village
of Gorham, New Hampshire, nearly
seven thousand miles and two thousand years
from the old Judean village of Bethlehem.
But the unique lighting effects in both places
at both times signify the same thing:
The most widely observed birthday the world has ever
known. The extraordinary Bethlehem illumination
attracted attention at a considerable distance.
Three wise men made a difficult journey
to the scene itself and thus achieved immortality.
"The star, which they saw in the east, went
before them, till it came and stood over where
the young child was." Now, in the White Mountains,
the lights burn again to welcome sons, daughters,
uncles, aunts, cousins, nieces and nephews
home for Christmas. This is the time of rejoicing
for shepherds and kings, farmers and clerks,
presidents and plumbers. In myriad villages,
myriad stars stand over where the young child was,
is and ever shall be. In jungle heat and
mountain gale, the many millions follow stars
on the night of the Nativity, full of hope that
once again the song of angels will be heard—
"Glory to God in the Highest,
on Earth Peace, Good Will Toward Men."

Photograph by Winston Pote 175